WINNING WITH DYSLEXIA

A guide for Secondary Schools

by Lindsay Peer
BDA Education Director

with additional material by Carol Orton

Published by the
British Dyslexia Association

ISBN 1-872653-06-5

Note to Readers

Throughout this book reference to she/he has been presented by the pronoun he for ease of reading.

British Dyslexia Association
Winning with Dyslexia
A guide for Secondary Schools

ISBN 1-872653-06-5

Published in Great Britain 1996

Copyright © The British Dyslexia Association 1996

All rights reserved. No part of this publication may be reproduced or transmitted in any form or by any means, electronically or mechanically, including photocopying, recording or any information storage or retrieval system, without either the prior permission in writing from the publisher.

Designed and typeset by Ibis Creative Consultants Ltd, Dulwich, London
Tel: 0181 766 6280

Published by:
The British Dyslexia Association
98 London Road
Reading
RG1 5AU

Telephone: 0118 966 2677
Helpline: 0118 966 8271
Fax: 0118 935 1927
E-mail: bda_dyslexia@cix.compulink.co.uk

CONTENTS Page

INTRODUCTION — 5
Chapter 1 - Definition, Characteristics, Needs — 7
- Overview — 7
- Profile — 7
- Working Memory — 7
- Phonological Deficits — 8
- Visual Processing Deficits — 8
- Handskills — 9
- Organisation — 9
- Personality Types — 9
- Self–Esteem — 9
- Across the Curriculum — 10
- The Multi-lingual Student — 12
- The Gifted Child — 12

Chapter 2 - Identifying and Assessing the Dyslexic Student — 13
- Reading — 15
- Spelling — 16
- Writing — 18
- Numeracy — 20
- Automaticity — 23
- **More Formal Assessment** — 24
- Medical Intervention: (a) Hearing — 24
- (b) Vision and Learning — 24
- Psychological Assessment — 25

Chapter 3 - Action – Practical Advice for Home and School — 28
- Differentiation of Materials — 28
- Spelling and Writing — 29
- Reading — 31
- Study Skills — 33
- Note Taking — 34
- Course Work — 37
- Revision — 37

		Page
–	The Examination	38
–	Computers and Dyslexia	39
–	Self–control of Learning (Metacognition)	42
–	Motivation	43
–	Relaxed and Alert	46

Chapter 4 - The Legal Framework   47

Bibliography   58

Appendix I   Recommended reading   59

Appendix II   Useful addresses   62

Appendix III   Publishers and suppliers of books and teaching materials   63

Skills Checklist

(A) General Identification	13
(B) Reading	16
(C) Writing	18
(D) Cognitive Styles in Mathematics	22
(E) Vision and Learning Difficulties	24

List of Useful Computer Programs   41

INTRODUCTION

This book is designed to provide the basis for a support system which will make life easier for secondary school teachers who deal with the full ability range of dyslexic adolescents in their classrooms. It is particularly for those who have no specialist training, and wish to know what can be done on a daily basis – and when and where to go for extra help when it is necessary. It is about good teaching practice: about teaching methods and approaches that would make it possible for all students to achieve success in their school career. The learning barriers and difficulties of a dyslexic student, a condition now recognised by the DFEE, is our area of expertise. Teachers will realise that many of the guidelines and methods suggested will support and enhance the learning of <u>all</u> their students, to a lesser or greater extent.

The teaching profession is a hardworking and caring one, but teachers have to work continually under constraints of time and resources. In those circumstances it will appear that some of the proposals for student support contained in this document are problematic. However, we all know that success motivates. A student with unacknowledged learning difficulties will not be successful, so he is unlikely to be motivated to learn. The sooner his difficulties are pinpointed and addressed, the sooner he will be successful and motivated to progress. Instead of diminished self–esteem with its associated behavioural difficulties, his self–esteem will grow with his successes. Therefore, time spent initially solving those difficulties will lead to less disruptive behaviour, fewer long–term problems for the student and a significant saving in time for the classroom teacher.

And time is at a premium for the secondary school teacher.

Unlike the one–class/one–teacher set–up that primary school teachers experience, teachers in secondary school may see four or five classes in one day and up to 120 different students each day. At this level teachers are concerned not with teaching the skills of basic literacy and numeracy, but higher level academic work with sophisticated language, complex ideas and a highly structured examination system at the end of it.

Many assumptions are made about the basic skills of the average 11 year old coming up to the secondary school – and teachers must move on as the curriculum demands. But what of those students who appear to be functioning well in some areas but badly in others? The form tutor will have noticed that there are some students in the class who are clearly not without ability in certain areas, yet are failing. Sometimes such students have notable skills and abilities – perhaps in subjects such as games, drama, debating, computers, mechanics. These students may have specific learning difficulties/dyslexia.

Teachers will be aware of the Education Act 1993 and the Code of Practice of Special Educational Needs, 1994 which require that they are able to (a) identify, (b) assess, and (c) support these pupils – but there is so little time in teacher training courses that teachers have often not had much training in SEN. They may be unable to put their finger on the student's problem. They are still asking "What is this Dyslexia thing and what else am I expected to do in my lessons?" They might see this student as yet another demand in terms of report writing,` and though he has 'great potential' he is a 'daydreamer', is 'just lazy' and 'could try harder'.

The problem of dyslexia is not just during school hours either – it goes home. Parents will be constantly asking themselves "Why can't he remember what I ask him?", "Why can't I make him do his homework?", "We sat up for two hours learning spelling and tables yesterday, why did he get them wrong today?", "Now it's foreign languages but we haven't got English right yet!", "He is so totally disorganised that he can't remember where he put his games kit!" "Why don't his teachers do something about it?!".

This book is just one part of the wide ranging support that the British Dyslexia Association offers parents, teachers, governors, head teachers, and authorities at all levels – and of course, young dyslexic people themselves.

Chapter 1
Definition, Characteristics, Needs

AN OVERVIEW

We describe dyslexia as: 'Organising or learning difficulties affecting language and working memory skills. Fine co–ordination skills may be affected in some cases. It is independent of overall ability and tends to be resistant to conventional classroom teaching. When untreated, there are significant limitations in the development of specific aspects of some or all of speech, reading, spelling, writing and sometimes numeracy – which may lead to secondary behavioural problems – but other areas of ability are unaffected.' [1]

The BDA estimates that 4% of the population is severely affected by a specific learning difficulty: that is, over two million people – of whom approximately 300,000 are in school at any one time.

Dyslexic people are not suffering from a 'disease'. Clearly, therefore, dyslexia cannot be 'cured'. However, with knowledge and understanding immense progress can be made and strategies acquired so that a dyslexic person can learn effectively and reach his innate potential.

PROFILE
Dyslexic people tend to fall into three groups:
(a) Those who have highly developed abilities in visual/spatial thinking and are less verbally able.
(b) Those who have highly developed verbal skills and are less good at skills demanding visual/spatial awareness.
(c) Those who have strengths and weaknesses in both these areas.

What all three types have in common, however, is a difficulty with literacy and/or numeracy. At first glance, it is easy to miss the differences. This may mean that the teacher teaches in a way that it is difficult for the student to learn. The student gets frustrated, and feels bad. It is very helpful for teachers to know how their students learn the most effectively.

WORKING MEMORY
The major cognitive weakness for these students appears to be in working memory. It is suggested that working memory is a system involving constituent memory

skills which are employed differently, depending upon the task undertaken. Many researchers have developed these ideas further and believe that **working memory is a process**, not a structure and as such can be developed.

It is generally concluded that working memory has the following main functions. These are to provide short-term memory systems for the five major senses so that new material may effectively be related to already stored information. In turn, information already in long-term memory can be utilised to facilitate perception and problem-solving. Finally, working memory allows the simultaneous performance of well-learned skills while new information is being integrated.

The particular interest of this to us is that dyslexic students have not acquired these skills and strategies from interaction with their curriculum and consequently find it difficult to use these skills to develop their literacy levels.

Practical examples of this may be the student who is able to decode 'competently' yet may not simultaneously comprehend the words. For example, the adolescent who is asked to remember a series of assignments whilst the teacher is talking about another subject might have difficulty in doing two tasks at once. He would be able to perform all the tasks individually, but his memory would be overloaded when told to retain larger amounts of information, resulting in difficuties with later recall. Another student who is struggling to spell, who has not been taught strategies, may not remember the spellings the following day in his test, or more likely, the following week, when asked to recall or use them in essay writing.

PHONOLOGICAL DEFICITS
Dyslexic children may have difficulties with any or all of the stages of learning to read and write. In normal development, children will recognise familiar sounds embedded in new words so that their vocabulary expands. Some are unable to do this. As young students, some may have experienced difficulties in rhyming and perhaps in spoken language processes. Others may have difficulties in auditory perception – perhaps in listening comprehension. Such students need to be taught specific learning strategies which will help them form the relationship between letter–sound correspondences: this is 'phonemic awareness'. Less severely dyslexic students may not have difficulties until they reach the more advanced levels of reading and spelling.

VISUAL PROCESSING DEFICITS
More recently, research has begun to focus upon visual processing deficits also.

The learner needs to use phonological skills in left hemisphere processing and visual skills in right hemisphere processing at different stages in reading development. Different weaknesses can lead to different types of literacy difficulties needing appropriate skills– directed training procedures.

HANDSKILLS

Handskills can also be a problem for some of these students. They may write slowly, reverse letters, form letters and/or numbers badly and sometimes write illegibly. Therefore skilled specific teaching methods are necessary for them to write well. However, some dyslexic students, even with weaknesses in the control, accuracy and speed of the pen may be extremely good artists and/or games players.

ORGANISATION

Self–organisation is an essential part of functioning in life generally. So many of these young people evidence difficulties in anything/everything from dressing when young to tidying their rooms, finding the appropriate textbooks and equipment, arriving at a lesson or giving their homework in on time. Their intellectual ability is by no means impaired, but the 'whole' problem of life needs taking in hand. 'Organisation' for many has to be taught.

PERSONALITY TYPES

Some educationalists believe that students should be given personality tests to discover how they learn and function most effectively. Studies have been made of personality–type assessments to highlight the four major functions: sense, intuition, thinking and feeling and have linked them to both extrovert and introvert types. Knowing their student's personality type, teachers could then adapt their assignments according to student needs.

Dr Ginny Stacey, a tutor of dyslexic students, says "A person will be highly motivated when his dominant function is fully engaged in a learning task (or in another activity). When the dominant function is excluded from a learning task, that task becomes a near impossible obstacle. Altering other details of the educational situation will not improve the learning ability."

SELF–ESTEEM

An area of great concern is that of low motivation and self-esteem. Misunderstood and/or mishandled dyslexic pupils can suffer significantly. Teachers have a great responsibility to nurture the self-esteem of all students, but particularly those pupils who have a 'hidden disability'. Some disabilities are easily identified, but dyslexic students look the same as any other. However, if they are not identified and understood they have the potential for suffering which may have devastating consequences.

Severe weakness in literacy acquisition is demoralising, leading in some cases to withdrawal or overt behavioural difficulties. There are great dangers in constant failure and teachers may need to build specific plans for motivation into their teaching.

ACROSS THE CURRICULUM
Such weaknesses affect the student across the curriculum. A weakness in memory will affect history as much as mental arithmetic and foreign languages. A weakness in spatial orientation will be evident in geometry and geography, as well as in an inability to navigate oneself around a school building.

Language difficulties for some students will be as problematic in numeracy as they are in literacy in that the language needed for maths is specific and complex and, if not understood, will not allow the student to develop the building blocks he needs to progress in this subject.

Some students will have struggled for so long with the reading process that they find reading tedious and soul destroying. Others may find the experience too tiring on the eyes to read more than is absolutely necessary.

Young students are required mainly to read simple texts for explanation, but by the time the student reaches GCSE level and beyond, the following skills will be demanded of him/her:

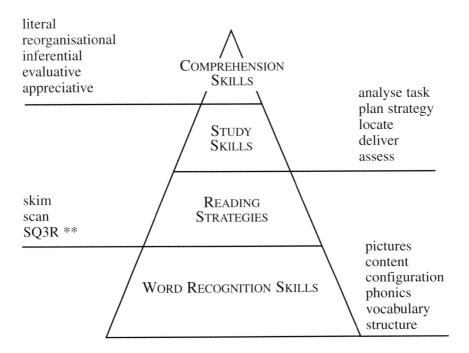

** Five easy steps to effective reading comprehension (see Chapter 3).

THE MULTI-LINGUAL STUDENT

The dyslexic multi-lingual speaker or the dyslexic student learning English as an additional language (EAL) will have extra problems to those already outlined.

When we learn a language as young children we firstly take an idea, structure it in language and then produce sounds. Once at school, the teacher then adds shapes to each sound and word and the reading process is launched. For the bilingual or multi lingual student there is double (or more) input: very complex linkages from this system which place a much greater load upon learning and recalling through working memory (an area which is known to be weak for dyslexic people).

For each additional language there will be extra structures, shapes, sounds and movement patterns. Added to this, there is the problem of different types of language used in different environments.

Where there is a dyslexia–type difficulty added to this profile, it is clearly problematic when attempting to define whether the problems encountered by the student who is acquiring reading, writing, etc. at a slower rate than others, are due to other language influences or to cognitive weaknesses.

Remediation for multi-lingual dyslexic children will be even more complex than for the mono-lingual student, and so we need to assess them as soon as possible in order to provide appropriate remediation at the earliest opportunity.

There is much concern about the situation of the multi-lingual/EAL student in our schools. Current assessment techniques seem to be limited in their breadth, leading to misdiagnosis of dyslexia within this group, and teachers often assume that students' difficulties are based on 'foreign' language interference alone. Dyslexia will affect all students regardless of race or number of languages spoken.

THE GIFTED CHILD

Not all students have all these problems. Many have outstanding abilities too. The average student with dyslexia may appear to be slow: the gifted student with dyslexia may appear to be functioning at an average level. As educators we need to observe such disparities of ability. With sensitive and knowledgeable handling dyslexic students will succeed. We need to deal with specific teaching skills rather than specific learning difficulties.

Chapter 2
Identifying and Assessing the Dyslexic Student

GENERAL IDENTIFICATION

Dyslexic students have different patterns of abilities and difficulties. Below is a checklist of potential weaknesses. If you discover a cluster, there is a need to investigate further.

Tick
<u>here</u>

- ...... Hesitant and laboured reading
- ...... Adding or repeating words when reading
- ...... Failing to recognise familiar words when reading
- ...... Missing out a line or reading the same line twice
- ...... Losing his place when reading, or still following with his finger/marker
- ...... Spelling a word several different ways in one sentence
- ...... Poor handwriting with badly formed letters
- ...... Very neat handwriting but written at a painfully slow speed
- ...... Difficulty with punctuation
- ...... Poor standards of written work compared with oral ability
- ...... Messy written work – ie words crossed out several times
- ...... Confusion between lower and upper case letters
- ...... Badly set out written work
- ...... Writing or talking a lot and losing the point of the question asked
- ...... Difficulties in note–taking in lectures
- ...... Difficulty in carrying out several instructions at one time
- ..... Difficulty in pin–pointing main ideas in a passage
- ...... Difficulty in using dictionaries, directories and encyclopaedias
- ...... Disorganisation of school materials

- ...... Difficulty in finding the name for an object
- ...... Unable to complete assignments on time
- ...... Difficulty in remembering sequences – e.g. tables
- ...... Confusion between left and right
- ...... Indeterminate hand preference
- ...... Difficulty in learning foreign languages
- ...... Excessive tiredness due to the amount of concentration and effort expended
- ...... Slow reaction time in answering questions
- ...... Difficulty in relating to others: inability to 'read' body language
- ...... Immature
- ...... Clumsy
- ...... Forgetfulness – sports equipment, lessons, homework, appointments
- ...... Misunderstanding complicated instructions
- ...... Being in the wrong place at the wrong time
- ...... Confusion of finances
- ...... Appearing to know much more than he can commit to paper

Generally the sort of young person you are looking for is the one for whom there is a discrepancy between oral and written ability, where you sense that something is not quite right – something upon which you can't quite put your finger.

Dyslexia affects all or some of the following skill areas:
> READING
> > SPELLING
> > > WRITING
> > > > NUMERACY
> > > > > AUTOMATICITY

READING
Primary teachers spend much time teaching the mechanics of the reading process employing various techniques depending on the policy of a particular school. If the teacher is dealing with a severely dyslexic student who is still having substantial difficulty reading by the time he reaches secondary school, one would hope that his needs would have been partially met and his abilities and difficulties documented. However, most of what is termed 'reading' is actually ensuring that students are able to decode a text. Adults 'listen' to students reading, but are they asking appropriate questions which allow them to see whether or not a student fully understands the text? Reading comprehension tasks are given, but are they of sufficient depth to see what is happening? Can the student comprehend the level of text books presented to him? Can he comprehend at speed? Can he keep up with the rest of his class?

Speed, accuracy and comprehension are essential pieces of knowledge that all teachers should possess regarding each and every one of their pupils. It is vital that history and science teachers, for example, know whether their students understand their texts and, if there are difficulties, know what to do about them. Does the student need extra time as he needs to re–read passages three or four times for information? Does he understand or can he even decipher long technical words? Much material is beyond the level of readability for many students – particularly those with special needs.

There are many tests on the market available to non–specialist teachers which give insight into reading speed, accuracy and comprehension of material read aloud.

There is far more to the skill of reading than just 'knowing the words'. We should perhaps adjust our reading approaches to the material at hand. For example, a newspaper will be read differently from a textbook, just as an 'A' level physics book will be read differently from an historical novel. For dyslexic pupils different strategies have to be taught – they will not just pick them up from the experiences of their curriculum.

As they move up the educational ladder more and more is demanded from students in the way of reading skills. (See diagram, p.11) If the foundation is not strong, there can be only limited development and reading skills will remain fragile.

Reading Skills Check list
1. Can the student discriminate between letters such as b/d, n/u?
   Or words   was/saw on/no?
2. Can he differentiate between words with only a single letter different, such as horse/house?
3. Can he differentiate between sounds – think/sink?
4. Can he recognise words that rhyme?
5. Can he break down words eg by syllables, and reconstruct them?
6. Does he recognise: sh/ch/th/kn/wr etc?
   ough/tion/sion etc.
   ae/ea/ou etc?
7. Does he recognise contractions: She'll, isn't?
8. Can he sequence letters in the alphabet? Can he use a dictionary etc?
9. Does he understand the concepts of word, clause, sentence, paragraph, chapter?
10. Does he understand 'explain, discuss' etc?
11. Does he have an understanding of tenses – did/has done/ had done?
12. Does he understand the significance of apostrophes?
    The girl's food – The girls' food?
13. Does he use correct plurals?
    Woman – women: fish – fish
14. Does he have a basic sight vocabulary? Is it appropriate to age/intellectual ability/experience?
15. Do punctuation markers mean anything to him?
16. What is his reading comprehension/speed/accuracy a) silently b) aloud? How does it compare with the rest of the class?
17. Can he skim/scan for information?
18. Can he use appropriate reading strategies for various types of work?
19. Can he reflect, think and create new ideas based on his reading?

SPELLING
It would certainly be wrong to suggest that all bad spellers are dyslexic. However, it would be fair to say that all dyslexic people have a weakness in spelling to some degree or other. Dyslexic students may mis–spell in various ways, depending on the severity of their dyslexia. It is very important that teachers remove as many

inhibitions about poor spelling as possible so that students do not get 'hang–ups' which limit the quality and quantity of their written work.

English is a complex language – and its vowel system can be extremely difficult for many to master. However, the impression that English spelling is unduly difficult arises largely because some of the most frequently used words in the language are irregularly spelt, although the vast majority conform to regular patterns. In a USA study (Hanna, PR et al 1971: *Spelling: Structure and Strategies* Boston) a computer analysis of 17,000 words showed that 84% were spelled according to a regular pattern, and that only 3% were so unpredictable that they would have to be learned totally by rote. It is a relief to know that there is a structure based on a rule system which is logical – and helpful – if taught to all pupils. It is not enough to allow pupils to read the rules for themselves – they need to be taught and re–taught them at all levels.

Until children have made the connection between the sound and the shape of letters, they will not spell, and unless they can articulate the sounds they will not be able to encode them. One would hope that, by the age of 11 years, all dyslexic students would have achieved these skills. In some cases, however, that is not the case.

One could identify some dyslexic students by 'bizarre' spelling such as 'brig' for 'cat'. More commonly found at the secondary level will be students who still write phonetically producing sentences such as 'Halo, wot a nis day for a picnic' or 'Please pars me my shows and socks'. We can read their sentences clearly, but this is unacceptable for written work at this level.

Other children may appear to do relatively well on spelling tests, but spell poorly when committing their ideas to paper in essay form due to a lack of automaticity. They may instinctively choose to use simple words to avoid such problems; they may spell the same word three different ways in the same essay – e.g. more, mor, moor; they may completely reverse words making errors such as 'saw – was' or reverse letters horizontally or vertically such as 'm – w' or 'b – d – p'.

It is more enlightening to observe a student's spelling ability in a passage of free writing as well as in a spelling test, and a comparison of the two would make interesting observation and guide us into building an appropriate educational provision for the student. (See Chapter 3 for examples of spelling rules.)

WRITING CHECKLIST

i) Checklist of writing characteristics of those students showing a great disparity of ability between written and spoken words.

(a) reluctant to write
(b) mainly uses short sentences
(c) uses monosyllabic words as far as possible
(d) repeats basic vocabulary, not daring to use longer more informative/technical language
(e) is unaware of different styles for different audiences
(f) tends to ramble – easily moves away from the point
(g) often gives good answers but not to the question posed
(h) lack of structure – beginning, middle and concluding paragraphs
(i) difficulty generally in writing in sequence
(j) difficulty in punctuation
(k) hesitation to use words difficult to spell
(l) may produce bizarre spelling (unusual at this age) or more likely use spelling that 'sounds' right eg mor, wos
(m) may reverse letters or words – eg b/d, m/w or no/on, was/saw
(n) difficulty in completing application forms/writing CVs.

ii) In handwriting, observe:
(a) how he holds the pen/pencil
(b) the comparative size of letters
(c) legibility/illegibility of handwriting?
(d) ability to copy correctly and/or at speed from a text book or blackboard
(e) difficulties with organisation of work on the page
(f) angle at which paper is held: is it awkward?
(g) whether he is generally hesitant about the whole writing process

These difficulties will appear across the curriculum. All mainstream teachers have a responsibility to note them and consider the implications when teaching, marking and testing.

iii) The following is a useful, easy to apply, quick test of writing speed which would show the speed of the pen on paper and allow the teacher to see whether his pupil can keep up with daily writing. (It does not look at rate of error nor age–appropriate level of literacy nor at a passage of free writing.)

Let the student copy three times (Chasty 1990) "The quick brown fox jumps over the lazy dog."

Age in years	Letters per Minute
7	28
8	36
9	45
10	52
11	60
12	67
13	75
14	13–15 words per minute
16	20 words per minute

The knowledge that your 13 year old pupil is copy writing at the speed of an 8 year old is meaningful to a class teacher who knows that free writing will be slower still. Such pupils are entitled to additional time (and, in many cases, other types of support) in school and external examinations.

Dyslexic students often have great difficulty in remembering punctuation markers in all their complexity when attempting to put together their ideas, grammatical structures and spelling. All these areas need to be taught in a structured, multi-sensory way for maximum effectiveness.

With regard to handskills, which also need to be assessed, it has been shown that approximately 13% of students do not have a dominant hand. Many dyslexic people fall into this category - which contributes to difficulties. Those who confuse left and right, easily reverse letters eg b/d, n/u, or words no/on, was/saw. Directional problems also slow down the writing process. (For this reason, young students should be taught 'joined up' writing when they first begin infant school. It certainly helps prevent reversals later.) Related difficulties, when young, of establishing where 'begin' and 'end' are on a page progress, when older, to difficulties in sequencing or organising ideas and words on a page.

Consider also the speed of movement of the hand for writing. Many students are unable to write at the speed demanded from them when note-taking from lectures, when copying from the board, or when writing in class or in examinations.

In such cases, there is every justification for extra time, for assignments to be photocopied from the teacher's notes, or perhaps to employ the 'buddy' system whereby a schoolmate writes/copies for the dyslexic student who is then free to concentrate on what is being explained.

NUMERACY

Numeracy is similar to learning a foreign language for many students – the vocabulary of mathematics being complex and unique. Sharma describes two levels of language:

(a) primary: classification and ordering of objects, quantity representing actions and collections, size, order, relationships, space, form, distance and time.

(b) higher level: the language of mathematics is used to help in conveying the results of logical thinking and reasoning. It is used in the collection, classification and organisation of data, and then in the analysis and interpretation of that information.

He points out that the student's native and mathematical language play an important role both in the conceptualisation of mathematical ideas and in the use of mathematical information.

If the dyslexic student finds the 'word' problems of mathematics complex, one ought to investigate whether it truly is a mathematical problem or one of language, or even of language processing. Take, for example, this question – said quickly, it is too much information to hold in short–term memory for effective auditory processing. Said with pauses, it is broken down and accessible: "Malcolm, Ruth and Angela/ each bought a sweatshirt/ at £19 each./ How much change would they get/ from £100?"

Also, the variety of vocabulary used to express the same idea is so broad that it can be complex for the student. For example ÷ might be verbally represented by divide, division, share, quotient. Or more explicity – How much will each cost? How much/many are contained within it? All this needs to be explained to the student.

Does the learner have a visual perceptual problem confusing, for example 2 with 5, 6 with 9, x with +? Are his abilities in spatial orientation and awareness sound? Can he keep his place on the board or in a book? Can he relate the two–dimensional drawing to the three–dimensional shape it represents? Can he turn the geometrical shape 90° to reappraise it?

There is also directional confusion. What of < and >?

Consider the directional problems involved in basic calculations. Addition, subtraction and multiplication are right to left, but division is left to right! And what of long division?

Question: Divide "4371 by 23"

Is it $23\overline{)4371}$ or is it $4371\overline{)23}$?

Complex long division involves carrying numbers and using both vertical and horizontal directions for calculation. If you do not remember where begin is or don't remember how to sequence numbers, etc. you will fail even if you appreciate the mathematical concept of long division.

Poor sequencing may make counting difficult, particularly backwards. The problem of 'left–right' awareness is as relevant to mathematics as it is to literacy. (Miles T & Miles E – 1975). The hesitation shown when reading numbers such as 9310 leads to problems. Is it 931– (nought doesn't count)? Might 81 be 18? Might 59 be 26? Can the student see the following sequences 9, 18, – , 36 or 2, 5, 3, 6, 4, – ,– ?

Place values are also an area for concern. Is the student able to evaluate the answer, - is 160.9 just as good as 16.09?

Sharma also talks of 'Mathematics Learning Personalities' (a) qualitative and (b) quantitative. Each of these groups of students need very different learning strategies if they are to reach their true potential in this subject. Sharma speaks of the 'mastery' of mathematics as being developmental and cumulative and having three basic components: (1) linguistic, (2) conceptual and (3) skills. Having assessed this, we then go on to ask if the teacher's style of teaching matches the child's way of solving a problem. If the student is predominantly a visualiser and the teacher is a verbaliser, the student is most definitely disadvantaged. Can the teacher therefore adapt to different styles?

In their book "Mathematics for Dyslexics: A Teaching Handbook" Chinn and Ashcroft [6] show the two different cognitive styles of learners – which they call the 'Inchworm' and the 'Grasshopper'. (See Table 2.1, page 22.)

Table 2.1 Cognitive styles of the inchworm and the grasshopper
(from - Mathematics for Dyslexics: A Teaching Handbook by Chinn and Ashcroft, published by Whurr)

	INCHWORM	**GRASSHOPPER**
I Analysing and identifying the problem	1. Focuses on parts, attends to detail and separates 2. Objective of looking at facts to determine useful formula	1. Holistic, forms concepts and puts together 2. Objective of looking at facts to determine an estimate of answer or range of restrictions
II Method of solving the problem	3. Formula, recipe oriented 4. Constrained focusing using a single method or serially ordered steps along one route (Rifle approach), generally in one direction – forward 5. Uses numbers exactly as given 6. Tending to add and multiply; resists subtraction and division 7. Tending to use paper and pencil to compute	3. Controlled exploration 4. Flexible focusing using multi–methods or paths, frequently occurring simultaneously (shot gun approach), generally reversing or working back from an answer and trying new routes 5. Adjusts, breaks down/builds up numbers to make an easier calculation 6. Tending to subtract 7. Tending to perform all computation mentally
III Verification	8. Verification unlikely; if done, uses same procedure or method	8. Likely to verify; probably uses alternate procedure or method.
Source Bath et al (1986)		

AUTOMATICITY

Automaticity is the automatic process of producing fluent work without conscious processing. Most people are able to focus on their ideas without thinking about, for example, spelling and punctuation. This would imply that the writing process has become automatic.

Whilst automaticity applies to all skill areas, its absence is most noticeable in the whole writing process. When 'spelling' has not yet become automatic many errors are made in the writing process. In effect, what happens is that the student is able to apply skills to strategies acquired, but can only perform them individually. Ideally, the student should be taught to draft his work. Initially he writes down his ideas with no thoughts of anything but creativity. When this is done, he then looks at punctuation. The third step might be to look at spelling. If a word processor is used the process is often more efficient. Creativity is greatly reduced if all efforts are being used on spelling and punctuation. This is an important consequence of lack of automaticity.

For automaticity to happen there has to be a transfer of skills which, for many dyslexic people, may take a very long period of time and only then with the help of highly specialised teachers.

What is the next step?
MORE FORMAL ASSESSMENT

MEDICAL INTERVENTION
(a) Hearing
The history of a student's hearing needs to be documented, if possible by asking questions of parents. It has been suggested that if students have suffered a loss of hearing even as early as 9 – 18 months they will not have learned to listen well and will need to be taught this skill. Implications will be for subsequent weaknesses in the general processing of language. This is noticeable, particularly in listening comprehension tests.

Many have a history of hearing loss particularly between the ages of 3 – 5 due to *otitis media* ('glue ear') and it is possible that this can lead to impairment in phonological development and also affect short–term memory. Research does not show which comes first, but it is helpful for an assessor to be aware of the background, before moving on to more formal assessment, and it is important that a current hearing test is carried out to establish that there are no residual hearing difficulties which could be impeding learning. Any evidence that points to intervention by language and communication therapists would be noted for the medical appraisal.

When the student is going for Stage 4 assessment, possibly leading to the acquisition of a Statement of Educational Needs, the medical doctor will be brought in to check the student's physical condition and to request tests of hearing and vision.

(b) Vision and Learning
For many years, teachers and assessors have requested that students have their eyes tested by an optician to ensure that there are no problems with sight which may lead to an inability to access literacy skills. Simple eye tests may well overlook the more complex visual difficulties which need more specialist assessment by an optometrist trained in this area.

A list of pointers here include:
(a) Signs of convergence/accommodation difficulty:
– complaints of blurred or double print – often momentarily
– reduced span of regard – only a small area of print is perceived at one time

- variations in 'blackness' of print noted – often clearing with a blink
- complaints of tiredness and fatigue with close work
- complaints of headaches after school and homework
- poor co–ordination in small ball games such as rounders and tennis
- slowness and difficulty in copying from blackboard
- deteriorating quality in written work
- variations in working distance – often becoming tired after periods of close work
- a tendency to blink, screw up the eyes and rub the eyes – usually during or after close work.
- complaints of 'rivers of white' on page of print
- complaints of print appearing blotchy
- reading tests that produce accuracy and speed scores that are below comprehension level.

In order to read effectively, one must also have the ability to be able to 'track' along the line.

(b) Signs of tracking difficulties:
- a tendency to lose place or line whilst reading
- a need to use a finger or marker to keep place
- tendency to miss out letters or words
- tendency to mis–order letters within words eg from – form
- tendency to confuse order of numbers when working on columns of figures
- confusion between hundreds, tens and units.

Once a student's difficulties have been diagnosed, a programme is set up to improve these areas of visual deficit. I would like to add that I have met many students who have not complained about visual difficulties as they assumed that everyone else also sees that way! Teachers should therefore be in the position to initially identify these students.

PSYCHOLOGICAL ASSESSMENT

If the student shows a cluster of difficulties, he should be assessed initially with the involvement of the school's Special Educational Needs Co–ordinator (SENCO). The problems may be relatively minor and may be dealt with by the building of an Individual Education Plan (IEP) as described in Stage 2 of the Code of Practice. [2]

However, if there is a suggestion that the student's problems are more severe, then the student may need specialist attention from LEA or other experts. At Stage 4 of the Code, an educational psychologist may carry out a full battery of assessments. This would fit the pattern suggested in the Code of Practice.

If the student's needs cannot be addressed at Stage 3, a full statutory assessment under the 1993 Education Act will be carried out. Questions may be asked covering the following areas:
- Parents' and student's personal details
- Parents' occupations
- Family incidence of dyslexia
- Previous help given – speech, occupational therapy, physiotherapy, psychological, remedial
- Health details – vision, hearing, general child development
- Memory skills
- Onset and nature of any emotional problems
- How parents and student view abilities and difficulties at school

Secondly, questions may be asked of form tutor and other subject teachers covering the following areas:
- Student's personal details
- Student's estimated potential: verbal/written
- Student's current progress: verbal/written
- Progress over recent times
- Student's behaviour and attitude towards friends and teachers
- Student's efforts
- A full description of student's abilities and difficulties

The in–depth psychological assessment ideally should cover the areas outlined below:

1 Ability	–	a full battery of verbal and performance tests
2 Perception	–	tests in perceptual skills
3 Memory	–	auditory, visual and visual–motor memory skills
4 Motor skills	–	looking at fine and gross motor skills
5 Laterality	–	self and others
6 Dominance	–	eye, hand, foot
7 Speech	–	receptive and expressive language
	–	auditory perceptual skills

8 Reading	–	single words
	–	contextual for comprehension, speed and accuracy
9 Spelling	–	both in standard test form and in free writing
10 Writing	–	timed writing – looking for:

        (a) spelling
        (b) punctuation
        (c) handwriting
        (d) organisation and expression of ideas
        (e) speed of production
        (f) grammar
        (g) sentence construction

11 Mathematics	–	oral and written calculations
12 Personality	–	where appropriate

Having completed the tests the educational psychologist should be in a position to show the disparity between the student's intellectual capabilities and potential and his production of work. This would lead to a meeting together with a specialist teacher and the class teacher or tutor, where an educational programme of work would be outlined for the student - an Individual Education Plan (I.E.P.). Parents should be brought into the discussions at the earliest possible opportunity, in line with the philosophy of 'partnership with parents'.

The student's progress must be monitored and a review system set up where targets should be seen to have been reached. The student's provision should be adjusted according to need as soon as possible. There will also be the possibility of provisions at examinations.

The details of examination provisions are updated annually. However, general guidelines to date would be for extra time, disapplication of spelling errors in all subjects except for languages, an enlarged examination paper if required, and use of a word processor if the student regularly uses one for his work. In more extreme cases there could be the option of a tape recorder, a reader and an amanuensis. Currently, none of these provisions can be granted without the recommendation of an educational psychologist and the approval of the Examination Board.

The earlier a student's problems are identified and an appropriate individual educational plan initiated, the quicker the progress he is likely to make.

Chapter 3
Action - Practical Advice for Home and School

DIFFERENTIATION OF MATERIALS

We have established that these students have both abilities and difficulties and may need to be withdrawn from the class for well–targeted help. We have looked at the benefits of the change of attitude and simple tests and guidelines for general use, and we have considered the effects of good versus inappropriate handling on self esteem. What can we specifically do to answer the academic needs of these pupils in the light of the Code of Practice?

Differentiation has been defined as: "... the process whereby teachers meet the need for progress through the curriculum by selecting appropriate teaching methods to match an individual student's learning strategies, within a group situation." [3]

The National Curriculum 1993 states that differentiation is "..the matching of work to the abilities of individual students, so that they are stretched, but still achieve success."

OFSTED look for differentiation during their inspections of schools.

But what does it mean for our dyslexic students? It is the recognition that these students may well be able to learn at an academic level, but that the strategies given to them for accessing that information must be specifically designed and administered.

Bearing in mind the learning profile in question, teachers should ask themselves the following questions:

(a) If this student has strong visual–spatial ability, is there a way I can present this material to best suit his/her learning strategies?

When presenting work, is it always essential for the pupil to have to write linearly? Could adolescents produce videos, cassettes, photographs, drawings, diagrams for some specific tasks?

(b) If a child is stronger verbally, could he use tapes, could he lead a debate/discussion on issues, use role-play - generally find ways to verbally demonstrate his thoughts and knowledge?

While this demands imagination and time on the part of the teacher, the results will more than compensate for this by producing pupils who are more highly motivated, relaxed and rewarded by their own achievements.

SPELLING AND WRITING

Teach the whole class the basic spelling rules – some ideas are listed below. There are students who do not need them, but many that do – and not all of them are dyslexic. (Many OFSTED reports have noted that schools do not get good results in spelling.) If these are taught in a logical order and students are encouraged to overlearn them, while this will not be the whole answer, it will enable most students to self–correct much of their work.

Spelling pointers

These are examples designed to show the beginning stages of the teaching of spelling. This list is far from complete but will give teachers some help regarding ideas available for the teaching of spelling. It is not designed to follow the rules of a structured course or replace the specialist teacher, but even for moderately

---

Helpful tips for teachers

a) When giving a word to spell, first dictate it then give it in a sentence eg "*There*. Please put the book over *there*. Write *there*." Ensure the student has understood the context.

b) Ensure he knows the difference between short and long vowels.
   (i) short vowels (*sound* of vowels) are indicated thus: ă, ĕ, ĭ etc
       example: h ă t
   (ii) long vowels (*name* of vowels) are indicated thus: ā, ē, ī etc.
       example: f ī n d

c) Ability to separate vowels is imperative for spelling. Not all pupils are aware of syllabification. If they cannot separate, teach them to place a hand under the chin and say a word. The jaw will drop once for each syllable.
   Example: e/l e/v a/t i o n.   Practise this with them.

d) Ensure each student knows the difference between consonants and vowels (remembering 'y' is sometimes a vowel).

e) There must be a minimum of one vowel in each word.

dyslexic students, as well as other students, it would be valuable. More seriously dyslexic students would need a structured, sequential multi-sensory approach with repetitive practice.

There are many spelling programmes available for mainstream teachers, with worksheets for practice, such as 'Alpha to Omega' by Dr Bevé Hornsby and 'Remedial Spelling' by Violet Brand.

Examples of Spelling Rules
Point 1:
Short vowels in one syllable words:
    short 'a'   as in hat, cat, bat
    short 'e'   as in bed, get, led
    short 'i'   as in hip, pin, rip
    short 'o'   as in hot, top, not
    short 'u'   as in cut, nut, up

Point 2
At the end of one syllable words ending with l, f and s the letter is doubled after a short vowel:
    ll   as in tell, spell, doll
    ff   as in off, cliff, puff
    ss   as in miss, stress, cross

Point 3   Magic 'e'. For example:
    (i)   a *(consonant)*e
        The 'e' on the end of the word is not sounded, but it makes the preceding vowel say its name, e.g. nāme
    (ii)   i(consonant)e, e.g. pīke

Point 4
    'ck' comes at the end of a one syllable word after a short vowel:
    eg   pick, stock, back

Point 5
    Use of 'k'
    Used before 'i' and before 'e' as in kiss, key
    (except in foreign words eg kangaroo)

Point 6
    'ch' digraph. The 'ch' appears after the 'n'
    as in pinch, stench, lunch

Point 7
    'tch' appears at the end of a one syllable word after a short vowel
    eg patch, hitch, crutch

Point 8
    Soft 'c' sounds 's' if followed by 'e', 'i', and 'y'.
    – face, decide, recent, bicycle

Point 9
    Soft 'g' sounds 'j' when followed by e, i and y
    – giant, germs, energy

Clearly, the dyslexic beginner and those with greater need will require a structured, sequential, multi–sensory approach. By the age of 11+ many students will be needing a "higher level" spelling scheme taught in a similar way. Areas covered employing such methodologies might be:

(a)   Syllabification
(b)   Doubling of consonants
(c)   Rules of prefixes, suffixes and root words
(d)   Alternative spelling rules, e.g. the choice of c/k/ck or soft 's' and soft 'c'.
(e)   Appropriate subject vocabulary:technical, subject–related words
(f)   Punctuation and grammar

There are many books that deal with the coaching of spelling in great depth.

READING

The level at which a reading programme is introduced will depend on the age, stage and ability of the specific student.

If he is a non– or almost non–reader, again I would recommend the use of a structured, sequential, multi–sensory programme before one can attempt to look at the texts presented at the secondary school level. Once reading has 'taken off' and differentiation has begun, success should begin to breed more success. Simple instructions can then be given, simple answers expected and interpretation of answers begun.

Multi-sensory programmes are generally used by specialist teachers on a one-to-one or small group basis. They employ the use of all of our senses to ensure the dominant senses compensate for the under-functioning of the weaker senses. We must learn through as many senses as possible. These programmes are taught in a highly structured and sequential pattern of over-learning.

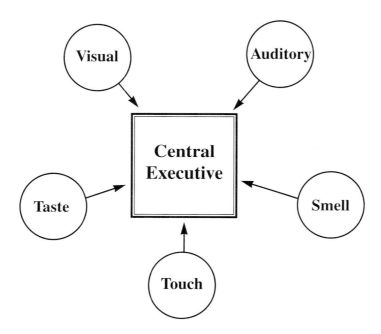

Once the student is reading, even if only at the level of a 9–10 year old, he will begin to demand more help, but will need material presented differently. He will need strategies, for example to facilite the extension of vocabulary; he will need to learn how to search for the sequence of ideas. Only then will he begin to show appreciation of the text.

At this stage we must take care not to be misled. First we must check that he is able to comprehend the text: the ability to read words is not enough. He must now go on to acquire such higher level skills as skimming and scanning, the ability to extract relevant information, acquisition of academic/technical languages. He will need to learn how to use dictionaries (the ACE dictionary being particularly useful to begin with) and encyclopaedias, how to form a bibliography, use directories and understand questions asked on forms. Life will take on wider horizons.

STUDY SKILLS

Organisation of time and self is the key to accessing the subject material, and enjoying school life. The student who misses deadlines and arrives late with the wrong books can create tension for both himself and the teacher. Dyslexic students are often disorganised and **need to be taught** how to help themselves within study skills programmes – all subject teachers can participate in this process. The student should be taught / encouraged to:

1. wear a watch and keep to a timetable
2. colour–code folders and books
3. make a list of assignments and deadlines
4. understand how a library system works
5. know where he can work quietly with few distractions
6. learn to prioritise.

Better overall organisation will allow more time to concentrate on developing specific skills – such as EFFECTIVE READING TECHNIQUES. Without these, many students will find the understanding of complex subject material very difficult. Lessons can be prepared in most subject areas requiring the use of the following well–established methods of:

SQ3R – Five easy steps to effective reading comprehension, as follows:

Step 1   SURVEY
(a) Glance over headings in chapter to see the few main points that will be developed. (b) Read the final summary paragraph, if there is one. This will show the core of discussion.

Step 2   QUESTION
Turn each heading into a question – this arouses curiosity and increases comprehension as well as bringing to mind information already known.

Step 3   READ (to answer that question)
Actively search for specific answers. Do this section by section.

Step 4   RECITE
Look away from the book to <u>say</u> the answer aloud. You may need to jot down a few key phrases. Then repeat steps 2, 3 and 4 with each successive section until the passage has been completed.

Step 5   REVIEW

Look over notes to get a bird's eye view of the points and their inter–relationships. Check your memory as to their content by reciting major subpoints under each heading.

Once these five points have been internalised and have become automatic, the student will become a far more efficient reader – faster, picking out important points, fixing them in memory. He will also find that tests become easier as he will be able to predict questions and answers and will feel altogether a more effective student.

Students should be given key lists of words to learn which indicate the meaning of complex sentences they are asked to explain. For example: discuss; evaluate; compare and contrast; summarise. Practice in questions incorporating these words will make for progress across the curriculum. How useful it would be for the economics/politics/ philosophy teacher to reinforce these words and for history teachers to bear this in mind when presenting complex comprehension exercises in source extractions!

NOTE-TAKING

Many students attempt to write copious notes from books and from teachers' lectures thinking that it is all necessary for revision. What they need is to be trained in how to extract the most important and relevant pieces of information and commit them to memory.

Essay writing, too, needs planning. Many of our students need to learn the strategies of 'attacking' what might seem to the non–dyslexic student a logical argument. Comments on their work commonly include:
- 'Plan your essay'
- 'You haven't addressed the issue'
- 'You've written pages, but not answered the question'
- 'Do paragraphs exist?'
- 'Re–read your work before handing it in' ...and the list goes on.

These students need to be taught how to address these issues. Even extra time from an examination board is not enough if they don't know how to tackle the points.

Mind Maps™ incorporate the use of colour, sketching and words, and can be adapted to every subject across the curriculum at whatever level. A typical mind map is shown opposite (see inside back cover for colour version).

Mind Maps™

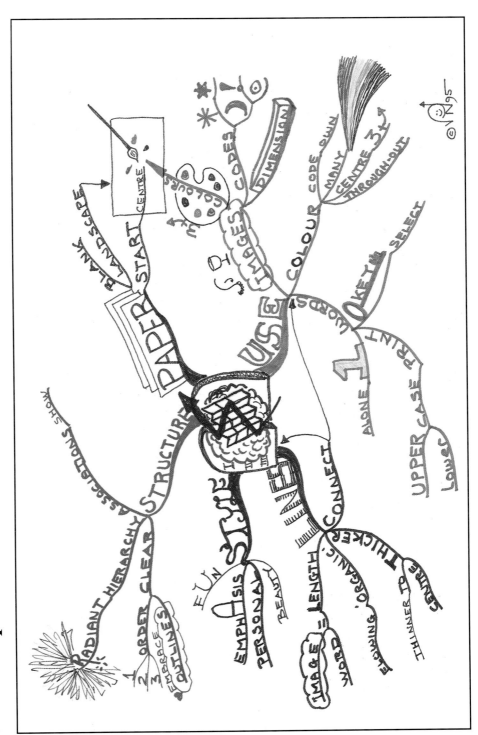

Students need to be taught how to plan out course work and take notes, as well as learn how to draft, plan and check their work. They will need particular help with the planning and techniques of revision as well as the preparation and techniques for exam taking (see Pollock and Waller) [4].

Organisation of timetables, books, homework and possessions is as problematic as the work itself and strategies will need to be taught to help overcome the difficulties and cope with the demands of the curriculum within specific time constraints.

Accelerated Learning™ methods are very helpful at identifying strengths and developing learning skills. Mind Mapping™ (for an example see page 35), brain storming, spidergrams and flow diagrams are other methods that can be immensely useful. Others may prefer linear plans. They do, however, need to be taught these methods to ensure the best use of them.

These students must be taught ways for organising their work. Coloured markers, underlining or numbering can be used to highlight headings and main ideas. If working in a linear fashion students should be encouraged to leave space around the groups of ideas so that extra notes can be added later.

The importance of references should be stressed, in particular as preparation for higher education, and students should be taught how to prepare a bibliography.

Poor readers should not be held back in mathematics – taped questions or oral instructions should be used.

The ordering of material is often problematic for these innately disorganised students and it is clearly the role of all subject teachers to develop these skills. For example, the history teacher could be working on the ordering of events and dates and be as effective at teaching sequencing skills as the English teacher, to whom the lot of teaching these skills often falls. Could the geography teacher work on the development of spatial awareness and organisation as well as the maths or English staff? And what of the sports staff? Awareness of personal and general space, directions and orientation; the control of a football or a basketball. Remember that until these larger skills are mastered students will find the more delicate ones – the 'paper and pen' skills – more complex.

COURSE WORK

With the school system as it is today, students at secondary level are expected to produce projects from private study. Some students find this easy – for dyslexic students this may be difficult:

1. They need the steps explained to them clearly – and often several times.

2. They have been known to write pages of irrelevant material. Careful monitoring is necessary to prevent this happening.

3. They need to be taught procedures for drafting material. This way they are able to get their ideas down on paper, without the tension involved in correct spelling, punctuation etc. Drafting might be divided into 3/4 stages: (a) creativity – first ideas down on page (b) correct punctuation (c) correct spelling as far as possible (d) print/rewrite if it is a very important piece of work. Move towards drafting in two stages and only once on the day of the examination.

4. They must plan out the technicalities of the assignment and ensure that they stay within the structure and criteria set out.

5. They should be encouraged to refer back to the guidelines and details of the question(s) on a frequent basis.

6. If the project has a practical component, such as laboratory work, ensure before commencing work that the student:
    (a) understands the safety regulations
    (b) reads and understands the assignment – he could explain it to you orally first
    (c) has the equipment ready to hand
    (d) knows where and how to enter results in an organised fashion

REVISION

Dyslexic students tend to have difficulty in committing the vast amounts of information they have learned to memory, due to deficiencies, as outlined, in the working memory system. As they see their peers working and reciting vast tracts, their sense of panic often grows.

Therefore:
1. They should be taught not to rote-learn, but to understand the material and know how to apply their knowledge. These students are generally good at this

which means they can succeed at one of the main objectives of any education system.

2. They must be encouraged to integrate the study skills techniques they have learned, such as Mind Mapping™, skim, scan and SQ3R.

3. A framework must be adhered to in terms of preparation time and subject matter.

4. If the student prefers studying in a group, each person could take responsibility for one area in depth and explain it to the others.

5. Short breaks should be planned in the revision schedule. Encourage the pupil to find his optimum work schedule eg study times of approximately 30 minutes with regular 10 minute breaks.

6. Find some past examination papers and use them in a timed situation at home in preparation for 'the big day'.

THE EXAMINATION
1. Ensure the student has the following equipment before the examination commences:
    (a) a watch
    (b) all equipment pertinent to the particular set of examinations

2. Remind the student to 'attack' the questions and prepare his answers – by using well–rehearsed methods of mind–mapping, spidergrams etc.

3. Prepare him to take his time to both read the instructions and the questions in depth.

4. Remind him to answer questions concisely and not to wander. Give him guidelines to timing.

5. At the end, check that he has:
    (a) answered the correct questions
    (b) corrected his work in terms of spelling, punctuation and general sense.

With understanding, support and the appropriate training in study skills over the course of time he should be better able to cope with his examinations and make a success of them.

Teachers must ensure that he is well prepared and makes good use of any provisions granted him with plenty of practice before the examinations.

Regulations and Guidance for GCSE Examinations are produced each year by the Joint Council for GCSE. These cover special arrangements and provision for candidates with specific needs. These arrangements, which are approved in advance of the examination, are to enable candidates who might not otherwise be able to do so to demonstrate their attainment. Candidates who may need particular arrangements include those with physical disability, visual impairment, hearing impairment, specific learning difficulties and candidates whose first language is not English.

COMPUTERS AND DYSLEXIA

Technology has introduced an alternative and valuable tool into the classroom. If the student's work is so messy as to be illegible or his handwriting so slow that it is ineffective, one might at this stage consider the use of a Word Processor. However, computers are not just for writing: 'Computers and dyslexia' is a whole world of its own and as we move into the next millenium, all those with a good knowledge of IT will be highly valued.

Many students are presented with a word processor and told to produce work. Clearly this is not a feasible proposition. Students need to be taught how to use the computer/word processor, how to type effectively and efficiently, use the spellcheck and thesaurus facilities, and how to select from and use the myriad of educational 'games' on the market. It will not be too long before all students can scan their material onto a computer which will read it to them. Their own voice will key in instructions on what to enter and print out.

Such machines have been developed but currently the cost is prohibitive. However, we are living in a technological age: schools should be encouraged to purchase such equipment to which relevant software could be added where feasible and appropriate. The provision of computers might also need to be written into statements of educational need.

Jean Hutchins, of the BDA Computer Committee says:
"Some schools are taking educational materials and scanning them onto sophisticated equipment. This is extremely beneficial to many of these students. They have shown that learning is aided across the curriculum. In the USA computers are used by many for accessing information. Students are able to help themselves in such a way that they need not disturb the teacher and the rest of the class – which is a very important factor.

"Dyslexic students want to be able to read and write as easily as the majority of their peers. They do not want to be 'different', but they need different provision in order to be the 'same'.

"We need the skills of reading, spelling and numeracy, and computer management and typing skills, in order to make good use of these support tools.

"The chart opposite shows some of the best programs for learning these skills (though there are others worthy of inclusion, and many of you could make your own version).

"This is not an either/or situation. Research noted in the UKRA booklet Literacy and computers: Insights from research (Ed. David Wray, 1994) pointed out that teachers who favoured structured programs also used framework software to apply the skills thus learned. We are always working towards that last column on the chart and independence for dyslexic people.

"When enquirers ask about computer programs, it would be so rewarding to be able to point them to a teaching program directly linked to the reading scheme being used with the dyslexic. If a Teacher Assessment or Educational Psychologist's report describes the current levels of achievement and the individual needs, we can suggest relevant programs. It is very important to choose appropriately – we cannot afford to waste even one moment of the dyslexic student's time, as they have so much catching up to do – and to co-ordinate all help that is being given.

"Dyslexic students have to learn many sequences which others pick up more easily. Some programs give the opportunity to use their newly learned reading and spelling and numeracy skills meaningfully in tasks. The second column of the chart shows some of these.

"Some dyslexic people, particularly adults, have worked through their early

List of Useful Computer Programs (From BDA Computer Committee listings)

	STRUCTURED LEARNING	SKILL DEVELOPMENT	HIGH LEVEL SUPPORT	INDEPENDENT ACCESS
Literacy	Linked with Scheme Alpha to Omega: WORDSHARK 2 SPELLING MADE EASY STARSPELL Bangor: all Xavier software Own Words COMPLETE SPELLER Specific patterns BREAK IN SUFFIXING Sequences Dictionary skills in WORDSHARK 2 DATADAY Reading speed SPEED READER Punctuation PUNCTUATE	Talking Books NAUGHTY STORIES Adventure programs FLEET STREET PHANTOM Short term memory Any Pairs/Pelmanism program Developing Tray TRAY Proof-reading PERFECT COPY Comprehension READ 'N ROLL Vocabulary Development WORD ATTACK 3 Typing Skills TYPE TO LEARN	Talking Gridbanks CLICKER PLUS Predictive Software PENFRIEND CO:WRITER TEXTHELP Talking WP TALKING PENDOWN WRITE:OUTLOUD TALKING FIRST WORD Automatic Speech Recognition DRAGON DICTATE Planning Tools THINKSHEET BRAINBOX Modern Foreign Languages LE MONDE À MOI	Word-processing and Desk Top Publishing Many - ranging from WRITER to WORD Portables DREAMWRITER Spellcheckers Computer-based in WP Handheld ELEMENTARY SPELLMASTER Thesauri Computer-based in WP Handheld POCKET THESAURUS Grammar Checkers GRAMMATIK
Numeracy	Number Patterns SUMTHING Good Drill & Practice TABLE ALIENS Telling the time/Historical time CLOCKWISE	Language of numeracy problem solving MATHS BLASTER MYSTERY Adventure with maths tasks WIZARD'S REVENGE CRYSTAL RAIN FOREST Investigations MATHS CIRCUS LOGO	TALKING CALCULATOR from Tandy	Calculators Computer-based Handheld from Texas Instroments Databases Spreadsheets

N.B. The Dyslexia Handbook (available from the BDA) lists a number of suppliers for the software listed above.

difficulties, but can benefit from help with organising their work, and strategies and equipment for dealing with residual problems. Keyboard skills and computer management will require specific tuition too. There is growing realisation of the value of being able to type fairly fast to make good use of word processing. Dyslexic students need repeated practice in using word processing facilities quickly and efficiently, and to have the instruction for reference in an easy form.

"The applications are exciting and very welcome. We must make sure that dyslexics of all ages have enough literacy and numeracy to make good use of them."

SELF-CONTROL OF LEARNING (METACOGNITION)
This is a vital step forward and may be defined as the higher level strategies of learning about learning. The student should have at his fingertips strategies from which he can choose to apply the most appropriate ways to organise his learning, leading to the extraction, storing, recall and use of newly learned knowledge and/or skills. They are transferable skills which affect learning at all levels and in all subjects. For example, I am engaging in metacognition if I notice that I am having more trouble learning A than B; if it strikes me that I should double-check C before accepting it as a fact; if it occurs to me that I had better scrutinise each and every alternative in any multiple choice type task situation before deciding which is the best one; if I sense that I had better make a note of D because I may forget it. All teachers should be encouraged to teach their students the value of self-control of learning [5].

Students should be able to apply the following questions to all of their work:
(a) Purpose: Why am I doing this?
(b) Outcome: What is the required end product?
(c) Strategy: What strategy should be used?
(d) Monitoring: Was it successful?
(e) Development: How can it be improved?
(f) Transfer: Can it be transferred to another skill?
When he can do this he is learning how to learn.

MOTIVATION

Let us take a look at areas of approval and approaches we could employ which would encourage motivation. The following is taken from a questionnaire based on research designed by Dunn–Rankin, Shimizu and King in 1969.

Adult Approval
1   Teacher writes 100 on your paper.
2   Teacher writes 'A' on your paper.
3   Teacher writes 'Perfect' on your paper.
4   Teacher writes 'Excellent' on your paper.

Competitive Approval
1   Be first to finish your work.
2   The only one that can answer a question.
3   Have only your paper shown to the class.
4   Have your paper put on the bulletin board.

Peer Approval
1   Students ask you to be on their team.
2   Friends ask you to sit with them.
3   Classmates ask you to be the class leader.
4   Friends ask you to work with them.

Independence Rewards
1   Be free to do what you like.
2   Be free to go outside.
3   Be free to play outside.
4   Be free to work on something you like.

Consumable Rewards
1   A packet of chewing gum.
2   A bar of chocolate.
3   An ice cream cone.
4   A soft drink.

Let us consider these:
Adult Approval –   How often does a dyslexic student get such a high grade? He might work extremely hard – have all the information and yet have his spelling let

him down. We must ask ourselves as educators what it is we are marking for. Is it knowledge acquired or is it the spelling of it? Some teachers for this reason will give two grades, others will ignore the written errors and simply mark on information. Immediate reinforcement.

Competitive Approval –
* *Be the first to finish work.* Who says that students have to do the statutory "X" number of examples? There is no research showing which number of sentences, examples, pages is the most effective for learning. Why not, then, let the dyslexic student do perhaps half the number of examples, get them correct and finish on time?

* *The only one that can answer a question.* Many dyslexic students are extremely knowledgeable, but find great difficulty in getting information down on paper. Direct questions that you know the student can answer so that he is positively and publicly reinforced. If you want several answers to a question eg 'What were the causes for the start of the second World War?', give the dyslexic student first opportunity to answer: he will be sure to have one answer at least, even if he can't remember them all. You might also clean the board whilst allowing him to formulate his answers. You could also make a private arrangement with him that you will only ask him a question if you stand in front of him first. That way he will not be stressed on a constant basis, will process at a pace he can cope with and, as a consequence, learn more effectively. Experience has shown that, once the stress is removed, in a relatively short space of time he will raise his hand of his own volition.

Peer Approval
* *Classmates ask you to be class leader.* Encourage the strengths this student has – perhaps in debating, if his oral skills are good, perhaps in games if he is a sportsman.

* *Friends ask you to work with them.* When grouping students look at this student's strengths and put him in a group where these skills are missing, eg if he is an artist/good at woodwork/has specialised subject knowledge.

Independence Rewards
So often these students are reprimanded for giving in work late; writing in a disorganised fashion; writing so slowly that they lose free/private study time. By making expectations realistic these students will succeed and will have the same rewards that others will receive.

Success encourages interest: repeated success builds confidence and, on a continuous basis, motivation. All teachers' aims therefore need to be: (a) to decrease frustration and failure and (b) to increase success. How is this to be done?

Do not ask the impossible, but always encourage intellectual stimulation.
The dyslexic student needs a highly organised and structured environment where he can work in a co–operative and attentive manner. Many instances could be quoted of students leaving the classroom with an excuse two minutes before it is his turn to read; others that regularly get head/stomach aches on a Thursday afternoon when they go to a lesson that demands perhaps oral tests of information memorised; or perhaps a teacher who has not noted that Susie writes twice as slowly as others and reprimands her for not completing work on time. Simply with a knowledge of these students' abilities and difficulties many problematic situations can be overcome, to the benefit of student and teacher.

What other ideas can be employed to reduce tension and increase success?
– Watch for dysnomia – word finding problems. Often these students know the answers but can't access the words quickly enough. It is intimidating when the teacher stands over the student, impatiently awaiting an answer. A relaxed atmosphere will encourage words/answers to appear quicker.

– Look, too, for the effects of 'mis–perceptions' on behaviour. Does the student get into trouble for deviant behaviour and yet genuinely does not seem to know what he has done wrong? These students need a programme designed to teach 'social skills' so that they can function effectively in a class, job and society as a whole. The whole class might benefit from such material, possibly through art or drama, or the individual student could receive help from special needs support staff.

– Can the student take notes as well as listen to the teacher? Generally not! Although he can do each on its own adequately. Research has shown this. A good study skills approach together with a 'buddy' system might be the answer.

– Watch for bullying at all levels – students calling others dumb, thick, dyslexic. Teachers ridiculing "Earth to Peter – Wake up!" as this would be immediately reinforced in the playground. The student will take it to heart and before long he's perhaps crying, anti–school, aggressive or maybe school phobic. Other students might not be outwardly aggressive, but internalise their problems, raising their stress levels significantly. All schools should have an anti–bullying policy. Ensure that it is enforced and do watch out.

Being aware of how to begin to help the student in class in his main-stream lessons takes no additional training and no extra money. With awareness and appropriate mangement of and reaction to his difficulties, you can put him on the road to a more secure sense of emotional well-being and at the same time remove a very significant barrier to learning.

RELAXED AND ALERT
Having given the student an awareness of who he is and how he best functions, confidence in his ability, strategies for dealing with the education system and control over the learning process, the final stage remains of teaching him relaxation techniques. This is again the issue of control, this time control of the body over breathing and awareness of muscle tension when faced with the tendency to panic in unfamiliar and stressful situations.

Control of the body, mind and learning processes lead to the control of life.

Chapter 4
The Legal Framework
by Carol Orton, Befriender Co-ordinator BDA

SCHOOL GOVERNORS
School Governors have specific responsibilities for students with Special Educational Needs under Section 161 of the 1993 Education Act.

These are that they:

a) use their best endeavours to secure that, if any registered pupil has special educational needs the special educational provision that his learning difficulty calls for is made,

b) secure that (for a student with a statement) his needs are made known to all those who teach him, and

c) secure that teachers in the school are aware of the importance of identifying, and providing for, those registered pupils who have special educational needs.
In addition Governors have to have regard for the Code of Practice for the Identification and Assessment of Special Educational Needs. They must publish information about their school policy for Special Educational Needs which must comply with The Education (Special Educational Needs) (Information) Regulations 1994.

While governors must plan and make policies for all students in their school, including all the students with special educational needs, the duty under the Act is to secure that appropriate provision is made for individual students which will meet their individual needs.

The Parents Guide to Special Educational Needs, published by DfEE, says "a student has learning difficulties if he finds it much harder to learn than most students of his age". If a student finds it hard to learn then the school should try and find out:
  what the student finds hard
  how hard he finds it
  why he might find it hard, and
  whether there is a way he would find learning easier.

Understanding the student is the key to tackling his difficulties in learning. This process of identification, assessment and considering provision should be detailed on the student's Individual Education Plan, and all teaching staff should be responsible for meeting the student's needs within their department.

Containing a student's difficulties is not the same as meeting his special educational needs. 'Meeting' is a more ambitious concept. If all a student's needs are fully met he can become an effective learner and achieve his potential. This should be the long term aim underpinning all special educational provision. The aims of education for pupils with difficulties and disabilities are the same as those for all students. The help they need in progressing towards these aims will be different.

The Code of Practice places much emphasis on the need to review all students with special educational needs by regular monitoring and evaluation. If the provision is not resulting in measurable progress it must be changed. No one expects schools to get it right first time – if they could then special educational needs might not exist at all! The willingness to search for the solution and employ specific and appropriate methodologies represents the main hope for students who find it, for whatever reason, so hard to learn.

The Code describes the sort of provision a school may be expected to make for a dyslexic student in para 3:62, without the need for a statement. This includes:

i   alerting all teachers to the student's particular needs, helping the student develop appropriate practices for taking down and recording information, adopting appropriate marking policies and promoting the use of such devices as personal dictionaries;

ii   structured literacy programmes and the use of multi–sensory teaching strategies for reading, spelling and number;

iii   monitoring the student's progress, consulting external specialists, including educational psychologists;

iv   seeking to involve parents;

v   exploring the possible benefits of IT, for example word processing and spell checkers, across the curriculum and at home;

vi monitoring the student's emotional and behavioural responses to his or her learning difficulties and providing help to reduce anxiety and enhance self–esteem.

It follows that such provision should be incorporated into a school's provision for dyslexic students.

STAGES OF INTERVENTION: STAGE 1

The Code of Practice proposes a 'staged approach' to meeting special educational needs. Some students have greater difficulties than others or have needs that are different and more problematic to meet. The amount and type of extra help they need must be driven by individual needs.

Many students with special educational needs will be accommodated at Stage 1 where their class teacher will be responsible for making provision with some advice from the SENCO. This is not so easy to organise in a large secondary school where class teachers will be subject specialists teaching the whole age and ability range and seeing each student infrequently.

Where schools have 'whole school policies' on Marking, Reading, Spelling, Study Skills, Language Development etc. it is possible to plan to meet the needs of many of these students using consistent methods across the curriculum. Each teacher must be aware of whether these strategies are adequate to meet the needs of individual students and INSET must equip them to focus on particular problems.

There must be clear channels of communication between all teachers to inform the review of pupils at Stage 1. These should be explained and published in the school policy.

STAGES OF INTERVENTION: STAGE 2

The more successful school planning is at Stage 1, the fewer pupils are likely to need support at Stage 2. Stage 2 is characterised by an Individual Education Plan (IEP). In writing an IEP the SENCO should consider what has not been effective or sufficient at Stage 1 and therefore what should be different. Diagnostic testing may give useful insight into the way a particular student is learning and where specific weaknesses lie. A careful analysis of work gives many clues on comprehension, spelling difficulties, memory and organisation. A good IEP may take some time to prepare but is likely to result in a better understanding of the student and therefore in a more focused and effective provision. Targets need to be set. The IEP should propose strategies that all staff can use. It is unlikely to be effective if special educational provision is regarded solely as the province of the Special Needs Unit.

Again, there should be clear channels of communication between all staff to inform the review and these should be described in the policy.

STAGES OF INTERVENTION: STAGE 3
Where a pupil is still experiencing difficulties and causing concern the SENCO should ask for external specialists to assess the student and offer advice as to how the school can further help him or her. This looking for help outside the school characterises Stage 3 of the Code. The external advisor, who may be an educational psychologist or specialist teacher, should advise the school on a new IEP. Since at Stage 3 the school is still responsible for meeting the student's needs the advice given should be practical and possible within the school's resources. The external advisor may, but need not, come from the LEA.

For all stages review dates must be set and parents informed what is happening and when the review will take place. Parents should know how they can contribute to the review process. At Stage 3 parents must be invited to the review meeting.

Students are expected to make progress as a result of the extra support offered. While it is understandable to say to parents 'We are doing all we can' the school must examine its range of provision and its suitability for individual students.

The Code of Practice says "Schools should not automatically assume that the students' learning difficulties always result solely or even mainly from problems within the student. The school's practices can make a difference for good or ill. The governing body ... should be alert and should examine the school's general policies and practices..." (2:19)

PARENTS
A student's needs may be such that withdrawal off-site may be appropriate at any stage of the Code. The DfEE offers the following guidance:

"Where a registered pupil, for example a dyslexic student, requires special tuition off–site and the arrangements have been agreed by the school, leave of absence may be granted and the absence treated as authorised. It is for the school to decide whether to agree to such an arrangement in the light of the individual circumstances, but in general one hour's off–site tuition per week might not be regarded as unreasonable." 'School Attendance: Policy and Practice on Categorisation of Absence' May 1994.

The Code stresses the value of information from parents and the student and strongly encourages a working partnership between school and home. It must be remembered that parents can give advice as well as receive it. Parents whose students have special educational needs may have had similar problems at school themselves. The school should not assume they are not interested or unwilling. They may feel uneasy in a school environment but they should be encouraged to participate. The school policy must describe how a parent can express their concerns to the school and contribute to the assessment and review process. IEPs are supposed to explain what help parents can give at home. It is important that parents are confident and able to give the help proposed.

When a parent first expresses concern that their child may have special educational needs their worries should be taken seriously and the student entered on the special educational needs Register. (2:71)

ROLE OF THE SENCO

An effective Special Educational Needs Co–ordinator is invaluable in a school trying to meet diverse special educational needs within a limited budget. Governors should be aware of the responsibilities involved in the post and should resource it accordingly. The SENCO is not simply a teacher with additional administration duties.

The SENCO needs to keep up to date on the learning needs of the whole range of special educational needs, including appropriate diagnostic testing and assessment and convey information relevant to individual pupils to the whole staff;

The SENCO needs to be aware of the whole range of teaching materials for such pupils and successful teaching strategies and provide training to all staff in using such methods. The SENCO may devise and support 'whole school policies' for meeting a range of needs;

The SENCO must be respected by all staff and able to communicate well with and advise teachers who will then be largely responsible for meeting needs in the classroom;

The SENCO must organise the administration of reviews through all the stages in such a way that the review informs the better understanding of the student and more effective provision. The information must be communicated to all staff.

In a secondary school it is unlikely that this role can be fulfilled if the SENCO has a mainstream teaching role. This is not to say that the SENCO should not teach but that his/her teaching role should be flexible and focused on meeting the individual needs of some pupils. The true worth of a good SENCO will be apparent in a more confident teaching staff and in the successful learning of pupils with special educational needs.

Although gifted students and those who use English as a second language are excluded from the statutory definitions of special educational needs the skills of the SENCO will be valuable in meeting their different needs.

THE GOVERNORS' POLICY FOR SPECIAL EDUCATIONAL NEEDS

Advice on the information required in the school's policy is found in Circular 6/94.

The policy must describe how the governing body "evaluates the success of the education which is provided at the school for pupils with special educational needs." The objectives of any special educational needs policy must be to improve the learning and raise the achievements of pupils with special educational needs. Simply evaluating the procedures described in the policy will not ensure a successful education. Some measure, possibly a different one each year, must be adopted that monitors the quality of learning of pupils with special educational needs.

The policy must explain how resources are allocated "to and amongst pupils with special educational needs". Resources are allocated to schools via formulae that are both pupil led, (the Age-Weighted Pupil Unit (AWPU)) and for additional needs, which vary between LEA's, but often include special educational needs. The formulae are supposed to be 'transparent' so that it is clear how much a school is expected to spend on special educational needs. So long as the school can show it is spending all its special educational needs funding effectively there should be no problem in asking the LEA for a statutory assessment if any student has such severe needs that they cannot be provided for from the schools resources.

It is straightforward to allocate resources to INSET, staff salaries etc. but not so easy to relate this to individuals or groups of students. The Governors should be aware, when setting the budgets, how the resources they allocate for special educational needs are expected to ensure effective learning for pupils. The policy should enable parents to understand how their student will receive the help he needs.

The policy must describe arrangements for the treatment of complaints from parents whose students have special educational needs. If parents' views are respected from the beginning their anxieties will be reduced. If good assessment and review procedures are in place, and the school offers a range of appropriate teaching strategies, there should be little reason for complaint. Since responsibility rests with Governors there must be a right to complain to the governing body at some stage. Parents have a right to complain to the Secretary of State if they feel that the governing body is acting unlawfully or unreasonably.

THE CODE OF PRACTICE

Governors must have regard to the Code of Practice but do not have to do exactly as it says. Para 2:64 summarises essential principles:

- provision for a student should match the nature of his needs;

- there should be a careful recording of a student's needs, the action taken and the outcome;

- consideration should be given to the wishes and feelings of the student;

- there should be close consultation and partnership with the student's parents;

- outside agencies should be involved, particularly at stage 3.

- Para 2:119 summarises the staged approach saying the school should: employ clear procedures to identify and register students whose academic, physical, social or emotional development is giving cause for concern;

- identify student's areas of weakness which require extra attention from teachers or other members of staff;

- develop, monitor and record, in consultation with parents and involving the student as far as possible, individual education plans designed to meet each student's identified needs;

- assess student's performance, identifying strengths as well as weaknesses, using appropriate measures so that the rate of progress resulting from special educational provision can be assessed;

- call upon specialist advice from outside the school to inform the school's strategies to meet the student's special educational needs.

These summaries describe essential procedures to ensure successful learning for pupils with special educational needs. Understanding different learning needs in a classroom will enable all students to reach their full potential. 'Purposeful and relevant' teaching strategies for such pupils are also highly effective for many other pupils without learning difficulties. The difference is that those who find it hard to learn cannot learn without such focused methods.

STAGES OF INTERVENTION: STAGE 4
Schools are expected to make a special provision that matches the needs of their pupils unless pupils have exceptionally severe or complex needs.

If the LEA needs to determine the provision for such pupils they will make a statement of the student's special educational needs. They will do this only after making an assessment of the student's special educational needs under Section 167 of the 1993 Education Act.

Some children will need a statement when the school, after trying to meet his needs through the stages of the Code of Practice, concludes that they cannot be met effectively within the resources available to the school. Yet others will not receive a statement. Their needs must still be met within the mainstream school.

The school can 'draw the LEA's attention' to a student possibly requiring an assessment. Parents can also request the LEA to make an assessment, under Section 173 of the 1993 Act. If parents make the request the LEA must decide whether or not to begin an assessment within 6 weeks of receiving the parents' request. If the LEA refuse to assess the parents can appeal to the Special Educational Needs Tribunal. If parents agree with the school's decision to request a statutory assessment it is therefore better if the parents also formally request the assessment themselves.

When the LEA considers whether 'it is necessary' for them to assess the student it will look for evidence that the student has significant or complex learning difficulties and that the school has taken "relevant and purposeful measures" in trying to meet those needs, through written IEPs and their reviews.

The Code describes the sort of provision a school may be expected to make for a dyslexic student in para 3:62. If, having used the proposed strategies, the student "has not made significant progress and/or the student's level of attainment is falling further behind that of the majority of students" the school should look towards a statutory assessment.

Attainment is not the sole factor to take into account. Para 3:50 of the Code says "apparently satisfactory progress may be found to fall far short of the performance expected of the student as assessed by his or her teachers, parents and others including educational psychologists.."

The LEA may enquire whether the school has allocated its resources effectively and whether the student's apparently weak performance may be attributable to factors in the school's organisation. It is only when a school, having done its best, cannot meet the student's needs that the LEA needs to begin a statutory assessment.

When the school is asked to give advice for the assessment it should describe clearly all the difficulties the student experiences. For a dyslexic student these would include difficulties with reading, spelling, working memory, perception, organisation and possibly difficulties with Mathematics, motor–control, language functioning, along with emotional and behavioural problems. It is better to describe the type of reading errors a student may make instead of simply giving a Reading Age. For example, a dyslexic student may reach an acceptable reading age by decoding text but will read so slowly and hesitantly that he will not gain any understanding from the text.

It is important to describe all the difficulties a student experiences. Part 2 of the statement, which describes Special Educational Needs, has been likened to a 'diagnosis'. A dyslexic student in need of a statement will have failed for some years at school. A good 'diagnosis' in his statement should ensure adequate and effective provision that will meet those needs.

It is also important to describe the provision that has been offered and why this is thought to be inadequate.

STAGES OF INTERVENTION: STAGE 5

Once the LEA has completed the statutory assessment they must consider 'if it is necessary' to make a statement. They may decide that the school should be able to meet the student's special educational needs after all and issue a 'note in lieu' describing the student's needs and offering guidance as to special educational provision.

Parents may expect the school to make such provision. The school should consider whether it can incorporate the advice into the student's IEP. The school has no right to appeal against the LEA's decision but the parents have a right to appeal to the Special Educational Needs Tribunal if the LEA refuse to make a statement.

When the LEA decide to make a statement they must send a proposed statement to the parents. The school will not receive a copy at this stage because the parents have a right to make representations about the proposed statement and to express a preference for a school, which may or may not be the same school where the student is at present.

Part 3 of the statement is the 'prescription' for the 'diagnosis' in Part 2. It describes special educational provision that must be made. It should normally be specific, detailed and quantified. It may describe provision that should come from the school's own resources as well as provision made or paid for by the LEA. It is the LEA's duty to arrange *all* the provision specified in the statement. The LEA has a power to visit the school for the purpose of monitoring the provison described in a statement.

Before the LEA name a school on the statement they must consult the governing body. The governors cannot refuse to admit a student solely because he or she has special educational needs. The LEA has a duty to comply with the parents' preference unless:

- the school is unsuitable to the student's age, ability, aptitude and special educational needs,
- it is incompatible with the efficient education of the other students,
- it is an inefficient use of resources.

In rare cases this might lead to a student being admitted even though the school is full, though this would normally be regarded as 'incompatible with the efficient education of other students'.

Parents have a right of appeal against the contents of a statement, including the school named on the statement.

The LEA must review the statement at least every 12 months. The LEA initiates the review and considers the report. The school makes all the arrangements but must follow Regulations 15 – 17, described in Chapter 6 of the Code. The school invites reports from all parties, including the parents. These reports must be circulated 2 weeks before the meeting.

The LEA may cease to maintain the statement but should only do so after extensive consultations with the parents. They must consider whether the student's progress would be halted or reversed if the provision specified in the statement were not made (6:37). The parents have a right to appeal to the Special Educational Needs Tribunal.

If the LEA ceases to maintain the statement the school again becomes responsible for meeting the special educational needs of the student, usually at stage 3.

This chapter is well summed up as follows:

"If this student doesn't learn the way we teach, can we teach him the way he learns – and then extend and develop his competences in learning?" (Chasty).

BIBLIOGRAPHY

[1] Peer, L: *Dyslexia: The Training and Awareness of Teachers,*
BDA Publication 1994

[2] Department for Education, 1994 – *Code of Practice on the Identification and Assessment of Special Educational Needs*

[3] Vicar, J: *Making it work – Ideas for Staff Development* , 1993

[4] Pollock, J. and Waller, E.: *Day to Day Dyslexia,* Routledge Press, 1994

[5] Flavell, J: *Metacognition* – Stanford University, 1970

[6] Chinn, S. and Ashcroft, R.: *Mathematics for Dyslexics: A Teaching Handbook.* 1993

Appendix I: Recommended Reading

Alpha to Omega (1993 4th edition)
Hornsby, B., Shear, F.
Heinemann Educational Books

Art of Reading, The (1989)
Ed: Hunter–Carsch, M.,
Basil Blackwell, Oxford

Becoming Literate (1992)
Clay, M.,
Heinemann Education, Auckland

The Dyslexia Handbook
Edited by Julia Crisfield
Published by the British Dyslexia Association

Giftedness and Dyslexia (paper 1994)
Lindsay Peer, BDA

Hickey Multisensory Language Course, The (1992)
Augur, J. and Briggs, S.
Whurr Publishers

Reading Development and Dyslexia (Selected papers from the Third International Conference of the BDA 1994)
Ed: Hulme, C., Snowling, M.,
Whurr Publishers

Remedial Spelling
Brand, Violet

Solving Language Difficulties (1971)
Steere, A, Peck, C., Kalin, L.
Educators Publishing Service Inc., Cambridge, Massachusetts

Spellbound/The Spell of Words (1981)
Rak, G.,
Educators Publishing Service Inc.

Changing Children's Minds (Feuerstein's revolution in the teaching of intelligence) (1987)
Sharron, H.,
Condor Books

Computers & Dyslexia: Educational Applications of new Technology (1994)
Ed: Singleton, C.,
University of Hull

Computer Support for Dyslexic Learners (1994)
Programme and selected papers of The Computer Conference 1994
University of Hull

Day to Day Dyslexia in the classroom (1994)
Pollock, J., and Waller, E.,
Routledge Press

Developing Spoken Language Skills (1993)
Browick, C., and Townend, J.,
Jones & Jones Publishers – for the Dyslexia Institute

Developing Literacy for Study and Work (1993)
Bramley, W.,
Jones & Jones Publishers – for the Dyslexia Institute

Developmental Dyslexia (1989)
Thomson, M.E.,
Whurr Publishers

Dyslexia: The Training and Awareness of Teachers (1994)
An example of best practice
Peer, L.,

Dyslexia & Mathematics: A Teaching Handbook (1993)
Chinn, S., & Ashcroft, R.,

In the Mind's Eye: Visual thinkers, gifted people with learning difficulties, computer images and the ironies of creativity (1991)
West, T.
Prometheus Books

Get Ahead (Video) (1992)*
Lana Israel
Buzan Centre

Help for the dyslexic adolescent (1985)
Stirling, E. G.
114 Westbourne Road, Sheffield, S10 2CT

Study Skills for Dyslexic Students (1993)
Stacey, G.,
Oxford Brookes University

Useful Dictionary
The Ace Spelling Dictionary (1986)
Moseley, D., and Nicol, C.,
Wisbech, Cambs, LDA

Use your Head (1989)*
Buzan, T.,
Ariel Books

Use your Memory (1989)*
Buzan, T.,
Ariel Books

*   Buzan products are available from:
Buzan Centre
Suites 2/3, Cardigan House
37 Waterloo Road, Bournemouth, Dorset

The BDA produces a publications list available by writing to them at the address below and enclosing a stamped addressed envelope.

Appendix II: Useful Addresses

BDA
98 London Road,
Reading, Berks RG1 5AU
Tel: 01189 668271

Dyslexia Institute
133 Gresham Road
Staines
Middlesex TW18 2AJ
Tel: 01784 463935

Dyslexia Teaching Centre
23 Kensington Square
London W8 5HN
Tel: 0171 937 2408

Dyslexia Unit
University of Wales
Bangor
Gwynedd LL57 2DG
Tel: 01248 351

Helen Arkell Centre
Frensham
FarnhamSurrey GU10 3BW
Tel: 01252 792400

The Hornsby Centre
261 Trinity Road
London SW18 3SN
Tel: 0181 874 1844

Scottish Dyslexia Association
c/o Sheila Airth
Unit 3, Stirling Business Centre
Wellgreen Place
Stirling
FK8 2DZ
Tel: 01786 446650

Medway Dyslexia Centre
1 The Close
Rochester
Kent ME1 1SD

NASEN
York House
Exhall Grange
Wheelwright Lane
Coventry CV7 9HP
Tel: 01203 362414

Appendix III: Publishers and suppliers of books and teaching materials

Accelerated Learning Publications
Aylesbury Road
Aston Clinton
Aylesbury, Bucks

Ann Arbor Publishers
P O Box 1
Belford
Northumberland NE780 7JK
Tel: 01668 214460

Better Books & Software
3 Paganel Drive
Dudley

LDA
Duke Street
Wisbech
Cambs PE13 2AE
Tel: 01945 63441

Letterland
Pictogram Supplies
Barton
Cambridge CB3 7AY

Whurr Publishers/Special Educational Needs
19b Compton Terrace
London N1 2UN
Tel: 0171 359 5979